MW00736526

#MANAGING YOUR VIRTUAL BOSS
tweet Book01

140 Ways to Make the Virtual Organization Work for You

By Carmela Southers

Foreword by Ken Blanchard

E-mail: info@thinkaha.com
20660 Stevens Creek Blvd., Suite 210
Cupertino, CA 95014

Published by THiNKaha®, a Happy About® imprint
20660 Stevens Creek Blvd., Suite 210, Cupertino, CA 95014
http://thinkaha.com

First Printing: August 2012
Paperback ISBN: 978-1-61699-098-5 (1-61699-098-8)
eBook ISBN: 978-1-61699-099-2 (1-61699-099-6)
Place of Publication: Silicon Valley, California, USA
Paperback Library of Congress Number: 2012939421

Trademarks

Warning and Disclaimer

Advance Praise

"Timeless wisdom on the timely topic of managing your virtual work manager. This book is a compact guide to the sometimes challenging business of ensuring you are successful in the virtual environment."
Joseph Bocchi, D.A., Marketing Manager, TechNiki

"This book provides very useful advice on how to manage the complex relationships in today's virtual workforce. Carmela's practical nature means that every hint will work for your success."
Lisa Cox, CPBA, CPVA, Manager of People Development, Aerotek, Inc.

"Self leadership is a critical skill for everyone. When you work at a distance from your boss, it is even more critical that you take the relationship lead. This little book's practical ideas don't just show you how to virtually manage-up, but through Carmela's way with words and sense of humor, it inspires you to take the initiative."
Susan Fowler, Co-author (with Ken Blanchard), *Self Leadership and the One Minute Manager®*

"As the organizational model and work structure is becoming increasingly global, it is very important for the employee and the manager to leverage and maximize the benefits of a virtual work force. This book provides a very pragmatic approach to working in this complex environment. The messages can provide a huge dividend to the employees and the organization for the time invested in reading it."
Hari Haran, President, Persistent Systems

"This book provides great insights on how to create and maintain a strong partnership with your remote leader. I have a virtual boss and will use the suggestions from the first tweet to the last. Carmela writes in a way that is compelling and helpful. Applying her practical tips will truly make a difference."
Sue Muehlbach, Manager, Performance Development, Delta Air Lines

"Even if your boss works close to you, everyone needs to be able to work with customers, peers, and project managers who work virtually. This book helps you take the lead in all your relationships. I wish this book had been available when I was starting out."
Michele Numssen, Global Commercial Learning Leader, Merck

"Carmela does a great job of capturing the essence of today's workplace. The book provides quick and relevant tips for building effective virtual work relationships and managing your boss. It's relevant for leaders and employees!"
Torrey Owens, CEO & Founder, Strategic Development Associates

"The ability to access information anywhere, anytime has expanded the way we do business, and the way we have to think about how we manage ourselves, our relationships, and our work. Carmela has taken the 'assumed' and brought it to the surface so the reader can see the benefit of building effective, open, and collaborative relationships with the boss and others. The end result will surely lead us to a reduction of conflict and mistrust that has been brewing since the idea of the 'virtual workplace' came to light. Thank you, Carmela, for putting together such a practical thought-provoking guide that will help anyone, whether you are (or aren't) working in a virtual workspace!"
Sharon L. Ridings, National Training Manager, United States Environmental Protection Agency

"If you want to help your employees win with their customers and their peers in our ever increasing virtual world, then buy Carmela's book today."
John Savoie, Regional Business Director, AstraZeneca

"Carmela Southers is right on target with terrific advice on how to 'win' as a virtual employee. This book should be a must read for every employee who wants to gain the flexibility to work off-site or from home! (Virtual bosses need their own copies, too!)"
Sioux Thompson, Financial Services Executive, Organizational Development and Learning

"Don't let a matrix structure in a global organization stall your success. This book helps you take charge of your career and all of your relationships in a positive way. Even the most experienced professional can benefit from these tweets."
Pamela Kaufman Wagoner, Chief Human Resources Officer, W.R. Grace & Co.

Dedication

This book is dedicated to my husband, Phil, and my children, Drew and Emily, whose patience, love, and humor bring me sustenance and joy.

And in memory of my mom, who always wanted a book dedicated to her. She has been my inspiration for life.

Acknowledgments

Thanks to:

- Maryann Brown, my color and graphics guru, editor, encourager, and treasured friend.

- Naomi, Sally, Ann, Chris, Barbara, Jackie, Sioux, and Pamela who push me to be the best I can be.

- Ken Blanchard, Pamela Kaufman Wagoner, Sioux Thompson, John Savoie, Sharon L. Ridings, Torrey Owens, Michele Numssen, Sue Muehlbach, Hari Haran, Susan Fowler, Lisa Cox, and Joe Bocchi for reviewing this book in its early stages and providing such kind support and praise.

Why I Wrote This Book

In the last twenty years, the workplace has evolved toward virtual work and technology-based communication. Since this transformation has been gradual, we often don't realize how much has changed in how we build relationships and accomplish work.

In my experience training and consulting with U.S. and global companies, I have met many leaders who meant well but struggled to manage remote workers. The skills they learned for face-to-face leadership did not automatically make them successful virtual bosses. These managers struggled to handle their emails and back-to-back meetings and forgot that effective workers needed motivation, encouragement, and personal connections to stay productive.

When I talk with employees, I find that many are frustrated because their team leaders, bosses, or human resources partners don't know how to provide effective management for virtual work. Employees feel their potential for career growth is limited because they can't get the visibility that being at the headquarters office allows, and their leaders either completely abdicate responsibility or micromanage. Instead of taking action, the employees end up feeling resentful, helpless, isolated, and alone.

My goal is to provide practical ideas to help all virtual employees get what they need to be successful.

Carmela Southers
Speaker, Author, and Senior Consulting Partner,
The Ken Blanchard Companies
www.carmelasouthers.com
carmela@sperlazza.com

How to Read a THiNKaha® Book
A Note from the Publisher

The THiNKaha series is the CliffsNotes of the 21st century. The value of these books is that they are contextual in nature. Although the actual words won't change, their meaning will change every time you read one as your context will change. Here's how to read one of these books and have it work for you.

1. Read a THiNKaha book (these slim and handy books should only take approximately 15–20 minutes of your time!) and write down one to three "aha" moments you had whilst reading it.

    "Aha" moments are looked at as "actionable" moments—think of a specific project you're working on, an event, a sales deal, a personal issue, etc. and see how the ahas in this book can inspire your own "aha!" moment, something that you can specifically act on.

2. Mark your calendar to re-read this book again in 30 days.

3. Repeat step #1 and write down one to three "aha" moments that grab you this time. I guarantee that they will be different than the first time.

After reading a THiNKaha book, writing down your "aha" moments, re-reading it, and writing down more "aha" moments, you'll begin to see how these books contextually apply to you. THiNKaha books advocate for continuous, life-long learning. They will help you transform your "aha" moments into actionable items with tangible results until you no longer have to say "aha!" to these moments—they'll become part of your daily practice as you continue to grow and learn.

As CEO of THiNKaha, I definitely practice what I preach. I read *#CORPORATE CULTURE tweet*, *#LEADERSHIP tweet*, and *#TEAMWORK tweet* once a month and take away two to three different action items from each of them every time. Please e-mail me your "aha" moments.

Mitchell Levy, CEO
publisher@thinkaha.com

Contents

Foreword by Ken Blanchard

This book is a virtual must-have for everyone who works remotely!

~Ken Blanchard
Co-author of *The One Minute Manager*® and *Leading at a Higher Level*

Introduction

Introduction

The world of work is changing and, like all change, it comes with the potential for both danger and opportunity. Although there are many skills required for working well virtually (organizational, technological, etc.), this book focuses on how to maximize your relationship with the individual who is the most critical (other than you) to your success—your virtual boss. If you work in an organization with a matrix management structure (as many of us do), these skills become even more critical as you manage your work with leaders, team members, and peers in both project and technical roles.

Principle: Although the title of this book may appear manipulative, my belief is that the most satisfying relationships both at work, and in life, are based on a win/win philosophy. The best way for you to succeed is to understand others' needs and motivations and to strive for solutions and actions that meet them.

Section 1
Understand Your Boss's Fears, Needs, and Priorities

Fewer layers of management, a larger span of control, and the virtual workplace make your boss's job more challenging. When your office moves into virtual space, many of the lessons learned from the face-to-face experiences of leading, partnering, and teamwork are no longer effective. Even if your boss attends great leadership training, most of the leadership techniques taught to managers are designed for management by walking around, not management via email. Your boss needs to feel informed, valued, and safe from the surprises that happen when he or she cannot see you working. This section provides clear guidance on how to ensure your boss is always your advocate when responding to inquiries from his or her boss, clients, peers, or the human resources department.

1

Approach virtual work by assuming that no one understands what you do and how you do it.

2

Your independence can make your boss feel that he or she adds little value. Show your appreciation for his or her support.

3

Bosses can't read minds; don't expect them to anticipate your needs.

4

Seek to understand others' needs, then meet both yours and theirs.

5

The best defense is a good offense. Never let your boss be caught by surprise.

6

If you can't reply immediately to your boss, explain your current situation (e.g., on a call) and when you will respond.

7

The most satisfying relationships both at work and in life are based on a win/win philosophy.

8

Bosses who micromanage actually believe they are helping you. Leverage that belief by keeping them involved.

9

Resisting micromanagement is futile. Jump ahead by initiating detailed briefings.

10

When you ask for help, also offer to help. No one likes being the only giver.

11

Bosses fear being asked for updates they can't provide. Keep your boss informed.

12

Although you may be a star, you are not at the center of your boss's universe.

13

Approach managing your boss as a challenge to your creativity, not your ego.

14

Get to know your boss's ideas, opinions, and thought processes so you can think his or her way when needed.

15

In some ways, positive relationships are easier to build virtually. You choose the timing and mood to project when you pick up the phone.

16

Learn your boss's boundaries for risk tolerance so that even when you are playing at the edges, you are still within bounds.

17

Ask your boss to explain the potential risks of an idea. This gets your boss thinking strategically, instead of reacting impulsively.

18

Every email, voice mail, and meeting counts. Make sure you have at least seven positive connections before your next negative.

19

Strive to be a low-maintenance worker. Your boss has enough to do.

20

Ask, "Since we work virtually, how would you like me to keep you informed of my progress?" Your boss's answer may surprise you.

21

Initiate a few actions that are good for your boss and organization. Brief your boss afterward to show that you can operate independently.

22

If your boss suggests a project that does not fit your desire and skills, outline a plan for accomplishing it with other resources.

23

Your job is to teach others the best way to treat you.

24

Ask your boss for a "buddy" or two to help orient you to a new team. This saves your boss time & provides new perspectives for success.

25

Asking your boss for a recommended mentor shows you whom the boss respects and whom you should emulate.

26

If you work in a matrix organization, each boss and team leader may require a different approach.

Section II
Blow Your Own Horn with Elegance

The best way to approach virtual work is to recognize that you are the only person fully aware of how well you perform your job. This section provides practical tips on how to market yourself as capable and successful without appearing self-focused or conceited.

27

Schedule a twenty-minute one-to-one phone call with your boss every week for updates.

28

Make sure your twenty-minute one-to-one call with your boss ends early. Your boss will appreciate the gift of time.

29

"What can I do to make myself easier to manage?" This question may take your boss by surprise, but it is a great surprise.

30

Sending an occasional link
to an article positions you as
a learner and a teacher who
helps others.

31

Spend time identifying your strengths, and then use them every day. Work will be easier and you'll be more successful.

32

Do not volunteer for everything—just the projects that leverage your strengths.

33

Never use a webcam unless
you are dressed professionally
from the waist up.

34

Visual or auditory distractions (like
a messy office or a barking dog) on
a video or conference call make you
appear unprofessional.

35

Everyone has setbacks. Reflect and market yourself based on how you turned a setback into a comeback.

36

Genuine praise in an email will be saved and used later. Blowing someone else's horn always provides an echo for you.

37

Consider yourself the strategic leader of your own projects. Use conference calls, emails, and reports to show the value you add.

38

Imagine yourself as always in the spotlight. Choose your actions and communication carefully.

39

Just state when you are available for a call. Never mention the kids, laundry, or contractor as the reason.

40

Note the phrases your boss uses in conference calls or emails to indicate priority. Use those exact phrases in your communications.

41

Never admit you are wearing pajamas when working from home.

42

Everyone loves success stories; share yours with an emphasis on the names of those who helped you. Your message will get forwarded.

Section III
Stay Focused on What Is Important

Working at a distance means losing those informal opportunities to align with long-term strategies or anticipate short-term crises that may affect your career. This section shows you how to remain a valuable team player by staying aligned with your organization's goals.

43

Regularly asking "How does this project help the larger organization?" positions you as a strategic thinker.

44

Never say "no" to your boss. Always say, "This is what we can do instead to achieve the goal."

45

When your brilliant idea is trashed, save it for recycling when the time is right.

46

The more you communicate what you are doing, the less you will be asked to explain what you have done.

47

Ask others, "What can I do to be more successful?" Then do it.

48

Take initiative. When informing your boss about new strategies, seek potential problems, not permission.

49

When getting negative feedback over the phone, make notes and say "thank you." Reflect later and choose your response when calm.

50

If you get a critical email, call to express appreciation and ask for additional detail. This usually startles people into helping.

51

It is easier to deal with jerks if they are virtual. (At least you have less time with them.)

52

If you cannot manage your own time and work, no one will put you in charge of someone else's.

53

One of the values of telecommuting and working virtually is that you get more flexibility in choosing colleagues. Choose them well.

54

Individuals like to talk. Interview colleagues in other divisions to build relationships and understand larger organizational issues.

55

Set up web-searching "alerts" for company or competitor news. Casually mentioning news items shows that you are "in the know."

56

Staying focused on the priority, even when your boss has not mentioned it recently, will be appreciated.

57

Add colleagues' photos to your contact list so you can visualize your teammates when communicating.

58

If the meetings you attend are not well run, ask permission to summarize to check your understanding of decisions made and tasks assigned.

59

Never multi-task while on the phone. Others can sense your loss of attention and may take it personally.

60

Multi-tasking during calls damages relationships.

61

When it comes to email, marking everything "urgent" makes you look disorganized and anxious.

62

When you respond to unimportant emails on the weekend, you don't teach dedication, you teach that your time is not valuable.

63

Deleting worthless emails feels like productivity, but it isn't. For real productivity, reduce the flow of incoming emails.

64

You will die with unanswered emails in your inbox. Get used to it.

65

Remember that working at a distance can keep you from getting sucked into the negativity of office politics.

66

Since you have fewer personal interactions, expect to be surprised by organizational changes.

67

"What has changed since we last spoke?" keeps you aligned with changing priorities.

68

Not being visible in the office sometimes keeps you from being a target.

69

Growing your career

means growing your

knowledge every week

by reading, interviewing,

searching, or reflecting.

Section IV
Develop a Reputation for Adding Value through Disciplined Communication

When people see your phone number on caller ID or your email address in their inbox, will they answer it promptly or ignore it? This section provides practical guidance to ensure your virtual communication is always perceived as adding value.

70

Act with intention on every

email, phone call, and

conference call.

71

If you cannot focus on the quality of your message, take a break and come back to it at a better time.

72

Despite popular myth, the quality of your email response is more important than its speed.

73

If three emails have passed and the issue is not yet clear, then pick up the phone.

74

Email is the easiest and least effective form of communication. Set clear email rules, or your teammates will email you into paralysis.

75

A phone or video call builds trust
in a way an email never will.

76

No one wants to be a failure.
Never criticize without suggesting
a path toward success.

77

Forget diamonds, emails are forever.

78

Write the action needed in the subject line of your email (e.g., "Need your input on idea").

79

People do not read lengthy emails. Make the first few sentences count.

80

Instead of copying your boss, forward the memo with an informative header (e.g., "Reply to Acme Inc. FYI: no action needed").

81

Always keep your calendar and voice mail up to date so others never wonder what you are doing.

82

Ask how people prefer to communicate and then communicate that way.

83

Always use a headset for phone calls.
You will hear and sound better.

84

Pay attention to how you sound
over the phone. Keep your voice
pitch low and calm.

85

In the virtual world,
your trustworthiness
may be more influenced
by your email's tone
than your character.
Always check for tone.

86

If the issue is sensitive, respond to an email with a phone or video call.

87

Never attempt to resolve a conflict or give critical feedback through email.

88

Leaving a phone message is always preferable to an email that might be misinterpreted. When in doubt, call.

89

Letting someone know you need time to think to respond to a message is better than having to retract a fast answer.

90

Listen for what is unsaid on a conference call.

91

If you are feeling defensive, follow up by phone and ask, "What am I missing about this situation?"

92

If you are unsure about your responsibility, send a quick email to restate agreements and request confirmation.

93

Breathe deeply and smile when you leave a voice mail message—smiles are audible.

94

People will love your conference calls if you arrange for them to end ten minutes early.

95

Set an automatic "delay delivery" email rule of ten minutes. This gives you one last chance to retract or edit the email.

96

Calling into a conference five minutes early shows that you are organized and you value others' time.

97

If your boss does not have agendas for his or her meetings, offer to create them. This shows leadership.

98

When sending a document for editing, specify how you want it edited (e.g., underlined, text replaced, highlighted, Track Changes).

99

Use personal names, a short personal greeting or comment, and emoticons to add a human touch to informal emails.

100

Every email is an opportunity to build trust, relationships, and reputation.

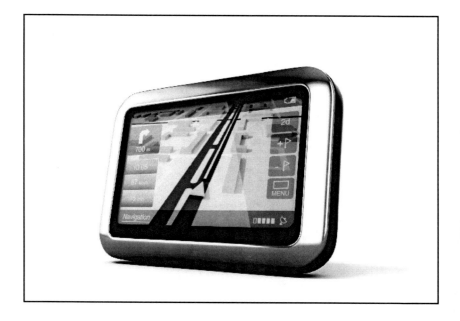

Section V
Moving Ahead from a Virtual Position

It is normal for virtual workers to miss out on opportunities to build a positive reputation and obtain the visibility necessary for promotion. This section provides tips for ensuring that you develop the skills, status, and network to be considered highly promotable.

101

People are hired for experience, not potential. Volunteer to get experience.

102

Leverage your flexibility as a virtual worker to quietly build your own professional network.

103

Virtual workers are often ignored when development opportunities are passed around. Make sure your development stays a priority for you.

104

Because you can't build hallway relationships, consider volunteering for a corporate charity or event.

105

Virtual success means influencing peers and bosses toward common goals.

106

The only way to be trusted is to be trustworthy.

107

Competitive relationships no longer work. Virtual work is built on trust. Everyone wins when trust is high.

108

Volunteering to capture and distribute meeting notes makes your email address more valuable.

109

No one cares about your success as much as you do.

110

Always find something positive to say about your boss to his or her boss.

111

Recognize that networking can sometimes be easier to accomplish when you work virtually.

112

Failure means you are stretching and growing. Report your failures to your boss by focusing on the lessons you learned.

113

Take advantage of free webinars, TED talks, blogs, and research available on the web relevant to your career field.

114

Remember that if your boss does not succeed, you will not succeed.

115

Leadership is about vision—even if it is only your vision for yourself.

116

As soon as you become an expert, network to train your replacement. If you are the only one who can do your job, you will never move up.

117

Demonstrate your leadership potential, even if it is with the charity drive, policy committee, or conference-call agenda.

118

Share what you have just learned with others. This positions you as ambitious, informed, and interested in developing others.

119

Your actions in your current position will position you for action in the next.

120

Leadership is personal.
Always treat people with
value and respect.

121

If you are comfortable in your current position, you are not trying anything new. Discomfort is necessary for change and growth.

122

Promotions are about relationships, and so are emails.

123

Do not be so easy to work with that you end up doing the work of others.

124

In virtual organizations and teams, roles often change or are unclear. Take the lead and define your role so that it works for you.

125

Being overworked today leads to resentment and burnout tomorrow. Pace yourself.

126

If you need a spur for innovation, look outside your discipline for inspiration. New ideas require new perspectives.

127

Becoming an expert in connecting virtually makes you a great resource for new projects and opportunities.

128

In the virtual world, that obnoxious team member could be your next project leader. Never make enemies.

129

Everyone has burdens and bad days. The rudeness of others is only a problem when you have not developed your resistance to it.

130

Blaming communication technology for your mistakes makes you look incompetent.

131

If you believe you are a victim, you are right. It is your choice.

132

A great virtual career is not about winning; it's about staying upright in the race, despite the hurdles.

133

Find, and be, a virtual mentor. Mentoring over the phone takes less time and effort.

134

Find a mentor in every age group. You will be amazed how different perspectives help your learning.

135

Feeling isolated is normal.

Staying isolated is a choice.

136

When you need to create or test new ideas, consider crowdsourcing with your contacts.

137

Consider becoming a "buddy" for foreign colleagues on your team. This keeps you up to date on organizational and team efforts.

138

Asking foreign colleagues to teach you some words in their language shows respect. Good-natured struggling makes you approachable.

139

Every quarter, make one new contact or offer to help in a project not in your area. New contacts bring new opportunities.

140

Recognize that sometimes, if all else fails, you might just need to get a new boss.

About the Author

Carmela Southers is a speaker, author, and senior consultant with The Ken Blanchard Companies. As an author of Blanchard's Teaming Virtually®, Leading Virtually®, and Leading Virtual Teams® programs, she is an expert on helping organizations, leaders, and teams succeed in the world of virtual work. Carmela travels in the United States and abroad training, consulting, speaking, and improving the effectiveness of remote leaders, teams, individuals, and organizations.

Books in the THiNKaha® Series

The THiNKaha book series is for thinking adults who lack the time or desire to read long books, but want to improve themselves with knowledge of the most up-to-date subjects. THiNKaha is a leader in timely, cutting-edge books and mobile applications from relevant experts that provide valuable information in a fun, Twitter-brief format for a fast-paced world.

They are available online at http://thinkaha.com or at other online and physical bookstores.

THiNKaha® Learning/Training Programs Designed to Take You to the Next Level NOW!

THiNKaha delivers high-quality, cost-effective continuous learning in easy-to-understand, worthwhile, and digestible chunks. Fifteen minutes with a THiNKaha book will allow readers to have one or more "aha" moments. Spending less than two hours a month with a THiNKaha Learning Program (either online or in person) will provide learners with an opportunity to truly digest the topic at hand and connect with gurus whose subject-matter expertise gives them an actionable roadmap to enhance their skills.

Offered online, on demand, and/or in person, these engaging programs feature gurus (ours and yours) on such relevant topics as Leadership, Management, Sales, Marketing, Work-Life Balance, Project Management, Social Media and Networking, Presentation Skills, and other topics of your choosing. The "learning" audience, whether it is clients, employees, or partners, can now experience high-quality learning that will enhance your brand value and empower your company as a thought leader. This program fits a real need where time and the high cost of developing custom content are no longer an option for every organization.

"This program has been very successful and in demand within Cisco. The vision and implementation of the THiNKaha Learning Program has enabled us to offer high-quality content both live and on-demand. Their gurus and experts are knowledgeable and very engaging."

- Bette Daoust, Ph.D
Former Learning and Development Manager, Cisco, and Internal Program Manager for THiNKaha Guru Series

Visit THiNKaha Learning Program at http://thinkaha.com/learning.

Just **THiNK**...

- **C**ontinuous Employee/Client/Prospect Learning
- **O**ngoing Thought Leadership Development
- **N**otable Experts Presenting on Relevant Topics
- **T**ime Your Attendees Can Afford – 15 min. to 2 hrs/mo.
- **I**nformation Delivered in Digestible Chunks
- **N**ame the Topic—We Help You Provide Expert Best Practices
- **U**nderstand and Implement the Takeaways
- **I**nternal Expertise Shared Externally
- **T**raining/Prospecting Cost Decreases, Effectiveness Increases
- **Y**ou Win, They Win!

CPSIA information can be obtained at www.ICGtesting.com
Printed in the USA
BVOW020254100912

299937BV00006B/1/P